Explore!

Shakespeare

Jane Bingham

First published in paperback in 2015 by Wayland

10 9 8 7 6 5 4 3 2 1

Dewey number: 822.3'3-dc23
ISBN: 978 0 7502 9404 1
Library eBook ISBN: 978 0 7502 8510 0

Editors: Victoria Brooker and Annabel Stones
Designer: Elaine Wilkinson
Picture Researcher: Jane Bingham
Step-by-step artwork: Stefan Chabluk

Wayland
An imprint of
Hachette Children's Group
Part of Hodder & Stoughton
Carmelite House
50 Victoria Embankment
London EC4Y 0DZ

Printed in China

An Hachette UK Company
www.hachette.co.uk
www.hachettechildrens.co.uk

Picture acknowledgements:
The author and publisher would like to thank the following agencies and people for allowing these pictures to be reproduced:

Cover: All images Shutterstock; p.1 (left) & p.26: BMCL/Shutterstock; p.1 (right) p.4 & p32: Shutterstock; p.3 & p.19: Shutterstock; p.5 (top): Wikimedia Commons; p.5 (bottom): Shutterstock; p.6: © Dean Conger/Corbis; p.7 (top): Shutterstock; p.7 (bottom): © Michael Nicholson/Corbis; p.8: Wikimedia Commons; p.9 (top): Shutterstock; p.9 (bottom): Shutterstock; p.10: Mary Evans Picture Library/MARK FURNESS; p.11: Andrew_Howe/iStockphoto; p.12: Wikimedia Commons; p.13 (top): Wikimedia Commons; p.13 (bottom): Andrew_ Howe/iStockphoto; p.14: Wikipedia Commons; p.15 (top): Shutterstock; p.15 (bottom): © Metro-Goldwyn-Mayer Pictures/Sunset Boulevard/Corbis; p.16: After Joris Hoefnagel/ The Bridgeman Art Library/Getty Images; p.17: © Look and Learn/ Bridgeman Art Library; p.18: © Ocean/Corbis; p.22: © Robbie Jack/Corbis; p.23 (top):© Look and Learn/Bridgeman Art Library; p.23 (bottom): De Agostini/Getty Images; p.24: © Look and Learn/ Bridgeman Art Library; p.25: Rosalind and the Old Duke, costume design for "As You Like It", produced by R. Courtneidge at the Princes Theatre, Manchester, Wilhelm, C. (1858-1925) / Victoria & Albert Museum, London, UK / The Bridgeman Art Library; p.27 (top): Mary Evans Picture Library; p.27 (bottom): Wikimedia Commons; p.28 & p.29: all Shutterstock. Other graphic elements throughout courtesy of Shutterstock.

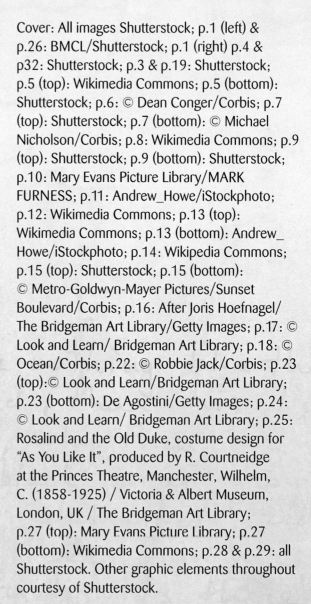

Contents

Who was William Shakespeare?

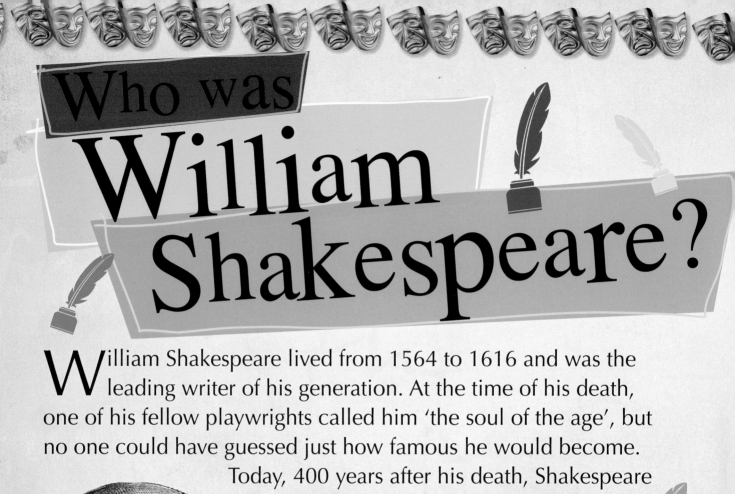

William Shakespeare lived from 1564 to 1616 and was the leading writer of his generation. At the time of his death, one of his fellow playwrights called him 'the soul of the age', but no one could have guessed just how famous he would become. Today, 400 years after his death, Shakespeare is the world's best known playwright.

Plays

Shakespeare wrote 38 plays altogether. His early works were comedies and histories. The comedies, such as *Much Ado About Nothing*, were full of mix-ups and confusions but ended happily. The history plays traced the lives of people from the past, especially the English kings. Later in his career, Shakespeare wrote tragedies, such as *King Lear* and *Macbeth*, which show the fall of a great man. His final plays include *The Tempest* and *The Winter's Tale*. They are full of mystery and magic.

This portrait of Shakespeare appeared on the title page of the first edition of his plays.

Shakespeare's plays have never gone out of fashion. In this painting, the famous 18th-century actor, David Garrick, plays the leading role in the history play *Richard III*.

Poems

Shakespeare was a poet as well as a playwright. He wrote several long poems and over 100 sonnets (poems with just 14 lines). The sonnets include a group of love poems addressed to a 'dark lady'. Nobody is sure who she was.

Shakespeare today

Shakespeare's plays are studied and performed in countries throughout the world. They have been made into films and adapted into operas, ballets and musicals. Even in the 21st century, Shakespeare can still amaze us with his exciting plots, convincing characters and playful language.

A Russian version of *Hamlet*. Shakespeare's plays have been translated into hundreds of languages.

5

Young William

William Shakespeare was born in 1564 in the small town of Stratford-upon-Avon. Tradition says that his birthday was 23 April. His father, John, ran a workshop making leather goods, such as gloves, purses and belts. His mother, Mary Arden, came from a wealthy family of farmers and landowners.

Growing up

William was the oldest of John and Mary's surviving children. (His parents had three daughters who died very young.) He had three brothers, Gilbert, Edmund and Richard, and a sister, Joan.

Very little is known about William's childhood, but it is almost certain that he attended the local grammar school. At school, he would have learnt reading, writing, arithmetic and some Latin. In his later teenage years, William may have worked as a schoolteacher or helped out in his father's workshop.

The grammar school in Stratford-upon-Avon has changed very little since Shakespeare's time. But today's lessons are very different.

The birthplace of Anne Hathaway, Shakespeare's wife. Anne's father was a wealthy farmer.

A married man

Shakespeare married in 1582. He was 18 years old, and his bride, Anne Hathaway, was 26. In 1583, the couple had a daughter, Susanna. Three years later Anne gave birth to twins, Hamnet and Judith, but Hamnet died when he was just 11. Shakespeare's early adult years are sometimes known as the 'lost years' because we know nothing about his life at that time.

Shakespeare in London

By 1592, Shakespeare had moved to London and started work in the theatre. According to one account, his first job was as a prompter, reminding actors when they forgot their lines. Another account claims that he looked after the horses of wealthy playgoers while they enjoyed the show.

By the time Shakespeare arrived in London, there were several successful theatres in town. This painting shows a theatre on the banks of the River Thames.

A great success

By the time he was 28, Shakespeare was working as an actor and a writer. But just as he was starting to enjoy some success, the plague broke out in London. In 1593 the order was given to close all the London theatres to avoid the spread of disease.

A wealthy patron

Without any work in the theatre, Shakespeare had no money to support himself. Fortunately, a very wealthy young man, the Earl of Southampton, had spotted his talent. Southampton acted as a patron for Shakespeare, paying him enough to continue his work as a writer. During this period, Shakespeare wrote two long poems. Both are dedicated to his friend and patron, Southampton.

Richard Burbage was a star of the Elizabethan stage. He played the leading part in many of Shakespeare's plays, including *Othello, Hamlet, King Lear* and *Richard III*.

The Globe Theatre was rebuilt in the 1990s. The modern Globe stands on the south bank of the River Thames, very close to the site of the original theatre.

The Lord Chamberlain's Men

When the playhouses reopened, Shakespeare returned to his work as an actor and playwright. He joined the actor-manager, Richard Burbage, in a company called the Lord Chamberlain's Men, and wrote an average of two plays a year for the company. By 1599, the Lord's Chamberlain's Men were so successful that they built their own playhouse, called the Globe.

Later years

As he approached his forties, Shakespeare started to slow down. In the ten years leading to 1601, he had written 16 plays, but over the next ten years, he wrote only seven more. By the 1600s, he was a very wealthy man. He owned a large house, New Place, in Stratford-upon-Avon, and in 1612 he bought a London house as well. Shakespeare died in 1616, at the age of 52, and was buried in his home town of Stratford-upon-Avon.

Shakespeare's tomb can still be seen today in Holy Trinity Church, Stratford-upon-Avon.

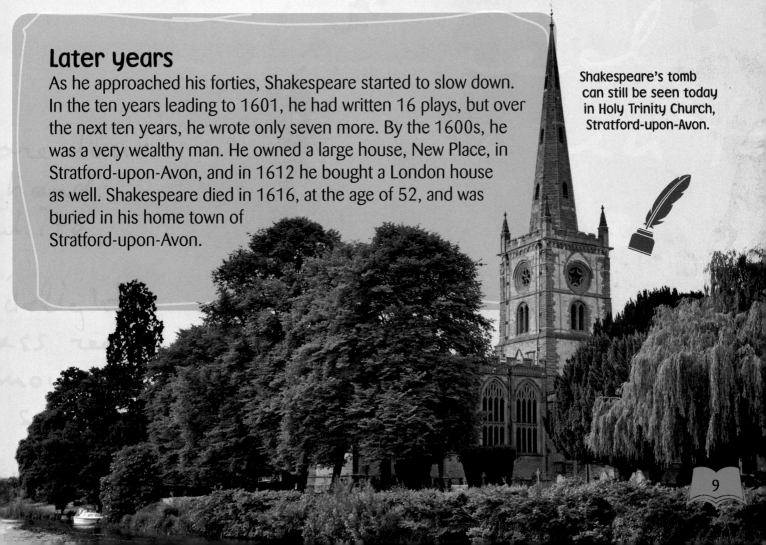

All sorts of plays

Shakespeare wrote four main types of play: histories, comedies, tragedies and romances. *Richard III* is a history play. It shows the rise to power of Richard Duke of Gloucester and his defeat at the Battle of Bosworth Field. King Richard is presented as a cruel monster, who committed terrible deeds to win the English crown.

Comedy

A Midsummer Night's Dream is one of Shakespeare's earliest comedies. It traces the adventures of four young lovers and a group of amateur actors, whose lives are controlled by fairies in a forest. Most of the characters mistake each other for somebody else, and they learn some valuable lessons about love. Like many of Shakespeare's comedies, it ends with several weddings.

This scene from *A Midsummer Night's Dream* shows Titania, Queen of the Fairies, with Bottom the carpenter, who has been magically transformed into a donkey!

Tragedy

The tragedy *Macbeth* tells the story of a brave Scottish general who is destroyed by ambition. In the opening scene, Macbeth meets three witches who predict that he will become King of Scotland. Encouraged by his wife, Macbeth kills the king, but is overtaken by guilt, fear and suspicion. He commits more and more murders and the play ends with his despair and death.

Macbeth prepares to murder King Duncan - the first of a series of violent deeds that will destroy him.

Romance

The Tempest is one of a group of romances written in the last few years of Shakespeare's life. It is set on an island, where Prospero, a magician, has been banished with his daughter. Prospero stirs up a storm that lands a shipwrecked crew on his island. Then he uses his magic to teach the crew some lessons and to find a husband or his daughter. At the end of this mysterious play, Prospero abandons his magic powers, and everyone returns to ordinary life.

Shakespeare's England

Shakespeare lived at the end of the Tudor age and the start of the Stuart period. During his lifetime, England became a rich and powerful nation and the English people felt proud of their country. Shakespeare helped to build a sense of national pride through his history plays. They trace the story of the English kings and queens, and show the Tudors in a very good light.

Queen Elizabeth I

When Shakespeare was born in 1564, Elizabeth I had been queen for nine years. She ruled until 1603 when he was 38. Elizabeth was a strong monarch who took a great interest in the arts. She encouraged writers, artists and musicians and invited them to the royal court. Many of Shakespeare's plays were performed for the queen, and she especially liked the character Sir John Falstaff.

Queen Elizabeth I was the last of the Tudor monarchs. She proved to be a powerful and inspiring ruler.

King James

In 1603, King James VI of Scotland inherited the English crown and was given the title of King James I of England. He became the patron of Shakespeare's theatre company, which changed its name to the King's Men. Shakespeare wrote his Scottish play, *Macbeth*, partly to please his new Scottish king.

King James I was the founder of the Stuart dynasty. He united England and Scotland in one kingdom.

A scene from *Henry IV*, showing the king's friend, Falstaff, surrounded by people of different classes.

English society

During Shakespeare's time, towns and cities grew rapidly and merchants and traders prospered. Noble families enjoyed great luxuries, but there was also widespread poverty. Shakespeare reflected the range of English society in his plays. His characters include kings, queens and nobles, but he also wrote parts for merchants, craftsmen, soldiers and servants. Women and children are often key players in his dramas, which were designed to appeal to people of all classes.

The wider World

People living in 16th-century England had a strong sense of the wider world. English diplomats, merchants and soldiers made frequent trips to France, Spain, Portugal, Italy and the Netherlands. Some adventurous seamen, such as Sir Walter Raleigh, reached North and South America, and Sir Francis Drake sailed around the world.

This map shows the known world in 1625, eleven years after Shakespeare's death.

Shakespeare's countries

It is not known if Shakespeare ever travelled abroad, but many of his plays are set in foreign lands. For example, the stories of *Romeo and Juliet* and *The Merchant of Venice* take place in Italy, while *A Midsummer Night's Dream* is set in Greece. Shakespeare also invented imaginary countries. The island in *The Tempest*, with its unusual creatures, illustrates his interest in strange and distant places.

The Italian city of Florence was the birthplace of the Renaissance.

The Renaissance movement

By the 16th century, a new movement in art and literature had reached northern Europe. The Renaissance began in Italy in the 1450s and was inspired by the classical culture of Ancient Greece and Rome. Artists and writers of the Renaissance rejected the medieval idea that human lives are controlled by God. Instead, they believed in the power of human beings to achieve great things.

Shakespeare and the Renaissance

Shakespeare was part of the Renaissance movement in Europe. Like many other writers, he was inspired by classical authors and often used their stories as a basis for his plays. The plots of *Julius Caesar* and *Antony and Cleopatra* are both drawn from classical histories. Shakespeare also explored the Renaissance idea of the power of human will. Characters like Macbeth and Hamlet struggle to decide what actions they should take.

Julius Caesar was very popular with 16th-century audiences. The play reflected a widespread interest in Roman history.

Shakespeare's London

London in Shakespeare's time was crowded, noisy and full of life. It had grown rapidly during the Tudor period and by 1600 it was home to around 200,000 people. Most of the city lay to the north of the River Thames, with the oldest streets around the Tower of London on the eastern side.

This map of London dates from around 1572. London Bridge was the only crossing point, so people often paid a ferryman to row them across the Thames.

A place of contrasts

The eastern side of the city was a maze of winding alleys, lined with shops, workshops and taverns. Families were squashed into small upper rooms, and dogs, cats, pigs and chickens roamed freely through the streets. With no proper drains, disease spread quickly, especially in the summer. By contrast, western London was a much healthier place to live. Here, the houses were built further apart and a row of palaces stood beside the river with beautiful gardens stretching down to the water.

London theatres

During the 1570s, theatre-going really took off in London, and several permanent theatres were built. By 1600, Londoners could visit the Curtain Theatre to the north of the river, and the Rose, the Swan and the Globe on the south bank.

Other entertainments

When they weren't busy watching the latest play, Londoners could enjoy a range of entertainments. Wealthy young men took part in contests to display their skill at billiards, fencing and archery. Poorer people held wrestling bouts and played rowdy games of football with dozens of people in each team. Cock-fighting and bear-baiting were popular spectator sports, and fairs arrived in town several times a year.

In harsh winters, when the River Thames froze over, a frost fair was held on the ice. The first recorded frost fair was held in 1608, when Shakespeare was 44.

The Globe Theatre

When Shakespeare's company built the Globe in 1599, it was the latest thing in theatre design. Shaped like a letter O, it looked like a mini-stadium. Inside, there was space for an audience of up to 3,000 people!

Watching the play

People of all classes flocked to the Globe. Wealthy citizens, such as merchants and courtiers, paid to sit in the galleries where they were sheltered from the weather. Gallery seats could cost up to six pence, but it only cost a penny to stand in the open yard. In Shakespeare's time, a labourer was paid 12 pence a day, so all but the poorest could afford to go to the theatre. Around 700 people – known as the 'groundlings' – squashed into the yard. The yard was sometimes known as the pit, and the groundlings were nicknamed the 'stinkards' because they smelt so strongly!

A cutaway model of the Globe, showing the three levels of seating.

On the stage

The actors performed on a stage that was slightly raised above the yard. Usually, they entered through doors or curtains, but sometimes they took the audience by surprise and appeared through a trapdoor in the floor! Some scenes took place on a balcony directly above the stage. In *Romeo and Juliet*, Juliet stands on a balcony while Romeo calls up to her from below.

In the hut

At the highest point of the theatre was a tiny room called the hut. It contained equipment for making sound effects, such as cannon shots or rumbles of thunder. Also in the hut was a large winch. This was used for lowering objects and even actors onto the stage. On the day of a performance a flag was flown from the hut: black for a tragedy, white for a comedy, and red for a history play. Before the play began, a herald stood at the door of the hut and played a blast on his trumpet.

In the rebuilt Globe Theatre, people can choose to sit or stand - just as the audience did in Shakespeare's time.

Make a model theatre

Elizabethan theatres were made from timber and plaster, with high, small windows, a large door and a thatched straw roof. Follow these instructions to make a simple model of an Elizabethan theatre.

You will need:

Three sheets of A4-sized paper or thin card

Glue

A ruler

A pencil

A rubber

Crayons or felt-tip pens

Scissors

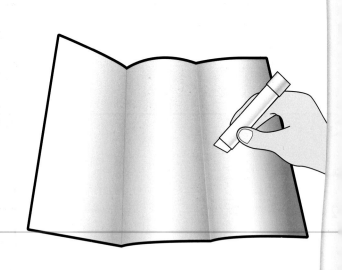

1 Fold each sheet of paper into three panels (like you fold a letter to put it in an envelope). Cover the right-hand panel of each sheet with glue.

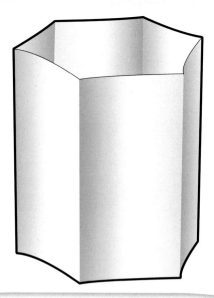

2

Glue the three folded sheets together to make a six-sided model building.

3

Flatten your model and use your ruler and pencil to draw two horizontal lines: one 2.5 cm from the top and one 1.5 cm from the bottom. Then draw a simple design of wooden beams, with windows and a door. Colour the top part yellow for the thatched roof.

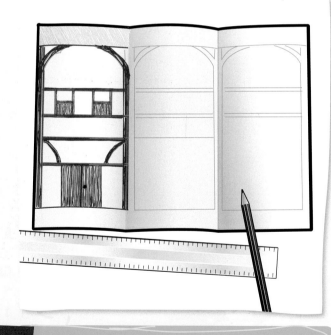

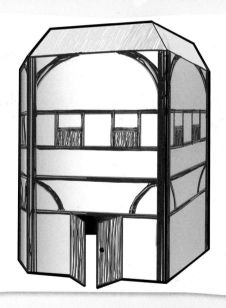

4

Bend your model so you can see one panel of your coloured design and two plain panels. Continue your design onto the two plain panels. Then bend the model again so you can continue the design onto the third plain panel. Colour in all three panels.

5

Make cuts along the six folds to where the top line starts. Fold the flaps in slightly and glue them together to make a sloping roof. Then make six cuts along the folds to where the bottom line starts. Fold the flaps inwards so your model theatre stands securely. Lastly, cut along the inside lines of the doors so you can open up your theatre!

Actors and playwrights

Working in the theatre was exciting but risky. If the audience liked your plays or your acting, you could become rich and famous, but if they were disappointed they booed loudly and even threw food at you!

Acting

Women in Shakespeare's time were not allowed to appear on stage, so all the actors were male. Boys played female roles until their voices broke. Then they moved on to acting male characters. Some actors became very famous, and writers wrote parts especially for them. Edward Alleyn and Richard Burbage took the leading tragic roles. Richard Tarleton was a brilliant comic actor, but he could not be trusted to follow a script!

In this modern performance of *Antony and Cleopatra*, Mark Rylance plays a female role – just as actors did in Shakespeare's time.

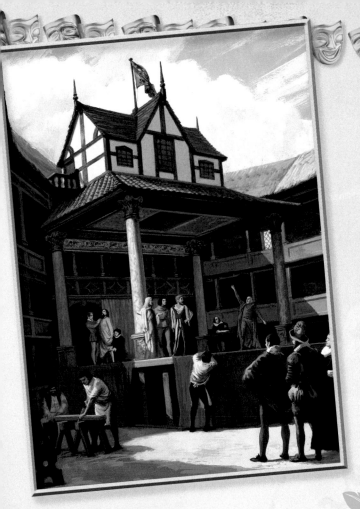

Touring

During the summer months, acting companies often went on tour, staging their plays in grand country houses. All their props and costumes were packed into chests and carried on carts from place to place. Touring was very hard work for the actors, who had to make long journeys on bumpy roads and often spent the night in uncomfortable lodgings.

Acting companies employed actors, writers, wardrobe keepers and carpenters. The carpenters were kept busy making special furniture to be used in the plays.

Writing

Shakespeare was one of many ambitious men writing for the stage. Some were bitter rivals but others were friends who worked together on the same plays. Most of Shakespeare's fellow writers have been forgotten, but a few wrote plays that are still performed today. Shakespeare's greatest rival, Christopher Marlowe, wrote exciting, action-packed dramas. Thomas Kyd and John Webster were famous for their revenge plays, featuring horrible murders. Ben Jonson wrote biting comedies that showed up the faults in his society.

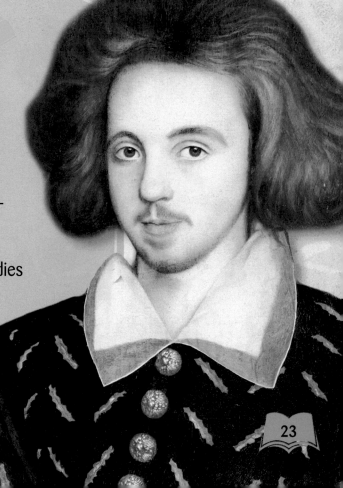

The young man in this portrait is believed to be Christopher Marlowe. He was stabbed to death at the age of 29 in a fight in a tavern.

23

A boy actor's day

This fictional diary entry is written by a boy in an acting company. It describes his day as he prepares to act in a play by William Shakespeare.

I get up early, feeling excited. Today, our company is performing *Macbeth*. I am acting the part of Fleance, the son of the Scottish lord, Macduff.

The rehearsal takes all morning, but at last it is our turn. We rehearse the scene when my father is stabbed to death and I escape. We try to make it as scary as possible!

While I eat my lunch of watery ale and bread I practise my lines. The prompter always gets angry when I forget them!

In the afternoon we get ready for the play. I go to the tiring room, where the actors are changing into their costumes.

I'm lucky to have a boy's part in this play. My friend Sam is playing Lady Macduff and his dress and wig are really uncomfortable!

The play begins at 2 o'clock. At first I feel nervous, but I soon relax. The audience screams in horror at the witches and roars with laughter at the porter's jokes. When we take our final bow, the groundlings go wild, clapping and stamping and cheering.

Our performance has been a great success, but there is no time to relax. Tomorrow we will perform a different play!

The diary entry on this page has been written for this book. Can you create your own diary entry as if you were a child living in Shakespeare's time? Use the facts in this book and in other sources to help you write about a day in your life.

Music and art in the theatre

Music was an important part of the theatre experience. A band of musicians sat in a balcony above the stage, and actors were expected to sing and dance as part of their performance.

Music for plays

Musicians played on instruments such as recorders, drums and viols (an early type of violin). They performed at the start and end of a show and in the intervals between the acts. During the play, trumpeters announced important entrances and the band accompanied any singing and dancing on stage. Shakespeare included many dances and songs in his plays.

In this modern performance at the Globe, an actor performs a lively dance. Some musicians can be seen in the balcony above his head.

A 16th-century performance of *A Midsummer Night's Dream* as imagined by a modern artist. There is no scenery and the actors wear very simple costumes.

Scenery and costumes

Theatres in Shakespeare's day did not have elaborate scenery. Instead, the actors performed on a bare stage and the audience used their imagination to picture a scene. Costumes were very expensive so the same clothes were used in many plays. Actors often wore or carried a prop to show their character. For example, a queen would wear a crown and a soldier would carry a sword.

Masques

By the 1600s a new kind of drama had arrived in England from Europe. Masques were short plays written in verse with dances and music and elaborate costumes and sets. Shakespeare's friend Ben Jonson wrote masques for the royal court with stunning costumes and sets designed by the architect Inigo Jones. Masques were fashionable amongst the aristocracy, but Shakespeare's plays appealed to people of all classes.

Ben Jonson wrote dozens of masques to entertain King James I and his courtiers.

Facts and figures

In 1603, when Shakespeare was 39, there was an outbreak in London of bubonic plague (also known as the Black Death). It killed 38,000 Londoners.

It is believed that Shakespeare played the ghost of Hamlet's father in a performance of *Hamlet*.

In his will, Shakespeare left his second-best bed to his wife. This was the only mention he made of her in his will.

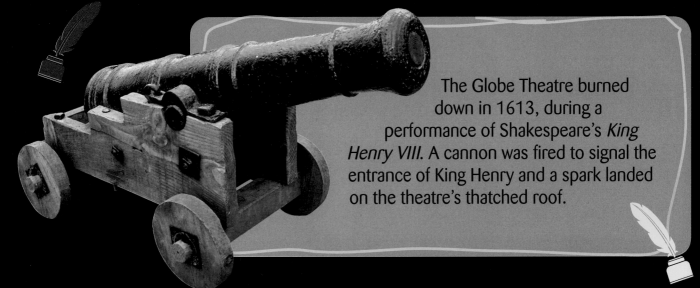

The Globe Theatre burned down in 1613, during a performance of Shakespeare's *King Henry VIII*. A cannon was fired to signal the entrance of King Henry and a spark landed on the theatre's thatched roof.

The first collected edition of Shakespeare's plays (known as the First Folio) was published in 1623. It was published by Shakespeare's friends, who wanted to stop people selling bad copies of his work.

Dozens of Shakespeare's phrases have become part of our everyday language. Here are just a few: laughing stock; heart of gold; naked truth; tower of strength; foul play; flesh and blood.

There are no records for what happened to Shakespeare between 1585 and 1592. One of his early biographers claimed that he was caught poaching (hunting illegally) and escaped to London.

Shakespeare invented over 1,000 words that have become part of the English language. For example, he was the first person to use: aerial; critic; submerge; majestic; hurry; lonely; and assassination.

Glossary

alley A narrow passageway or lane between buildings.

amateur Someone who is not paid for what he or she does.

banish To send someone away from a country as a punishment.

bear-baiting The sport of teasing bears to make them attack.

classical To do with or copied from the culture of Ancient Greece or Rome.

comedy A play that is meant to make an audience laugh.

courtier Someone who works at a royal court and advises a king or queen.

culture Writing, art and music.

diplomat Someone who represents his or her country in a foreign land.

edition A published book.

fictional Made-up or invented.

generation All the people who are born at about the same time.

grammar school A type of secondary school.

groundling An Elizabethan slang name for someone who stands in the yard to watch a play.

herald A person who announces official news or the beginning of something.

monarch A king or queen.

phrase A small group of words.

plague A serious disease that spreads easily.

playwright Someone who writes plays.

prompter Someone who reminds the actors when they forget their words.

prop A small object used by actors on stage. Swords and cups are props.

role A part played by an actor.

society People who live together and share the same customs and laws.

tavern An inn or pub.

thatched Made from straw.

tiring room The room in an Elizabethan theatre where the actors put on their costumes.

tragedy A play that deals with sad events and has an unhappy ending.

winch A machine used for lifting heavy objects.

Further reading

William Shakespeare (Extraordinary Lives),
Peter Hicks (Wayland, 2013)

The Shakespeare Stories (16-book boxed set),
(Hachette Children's Books, 2010)

Tudor Times (Craft Box),
Jillian Powell (Wayland, 2014)

Websites

http://www.bbc.co.uk/schools/primaryhistory/famouspeople/william_shakespeare/
A BBC website for children, with features on the young Shakespeare, Shakespeare in
London and plays in Shakespeare's time. The site includes fun facts, a quiz and a game.

http://news.bbc.co.uk/cbbcnews/hi/newsid_3530000/newsid_3539000/3539058.stm
A short guide to Shakespeare, with sections on words and insults!

http://www.folger.edu/Content/Teach-and-Learn/Shakespeare-for-Kids/
A website for children produced by the Folger Shakespeare Library in Washington, DC.
It includes puzzles and challenges, a game of 'guess the character', and a feature on
'weird words'.

http://www.shakespearesglobe.com/about-us/history-of-the-globe/shakespeare
A history of Shakespeare's Globe Theatre, from the website of the rebuilt Globe Theatre
in London. The Globe Theatre website includes a video tour of the theatre.

Index